LIQUOR LICENCE

PUNCH
on Booze

Edited by William Hewison

A PUNCH BOOK

Published in association with

GRAFTON BOOKS

A Division of the Collins Publishing Group

LONDON GLASGOW
TORONTO SYDNEY AUCKLAND

Grafton Books
A Division of the Collins Publishing Group
8 Grafton Street, London W1X 3LA

Published by Grafton Books 1986

Introduction and selection © Punch Publications Limited 1986

British Library Cataloguing in Publication Data

Liquor licence : Punch on booze.
1. Drinking of alcoholic beverages –
Caricatures and cartoons 2. English wit and humor, Pictorial
I. Hewison, William II. Punch 741.5'942 NC 1479

ISBN 0-246-13059-8

Printed in Great Britain by William Collins Sons & Co. Ltd, Glasgow

Introduction

There are drunks and there are drunks. Some are completely sloshed and legless, some are ready to scrap with any man in the house, some are just a shade tipsy and struggling to disguise it. And there are all the other conditions in between. So how does a cartoonist draw each of these characters to make it clear he's going for one type and none of the others? Not too many problems over the totally inebriated or even the fighting boozer, but that *slightly* drunk citizen is a trickier task altogether.

What our cartoonist has to do is present the fellow carrying on normally – standing or sitting or walking – then add those little signals which give the game away. The eyes should be half closed. The hair is not ruffled but one or two strands are sticking up, Iroquois fashion. There is usually a benign, sometimes idiotic, smile scrawled across the face. The tie is slightly loose and slightly askew. And occasionally, to press the point home, the cartoonist, ever ready to use all the tools of his trade, will add that touch of cartoon symbolism – the little swarm of bubbles floating round the tipsy man's head. All these pictorial indications of having had one too many, whether based on real observation or second-hand borrowings from other gag men, are absolutely necessary should the cartoonist need to present a very precise character to the reader. For it's got to be remembered that cartoons are riddles, and the clarity of that character could be one of a number of clues from which the reader has to make the final connection if he's going to get the joke.

Now don't run away with the idea that all the cartoons in this collection are about drunks and what they get up to; they are there, of course, tethered to the bars and tangled in the streets, but the net has been cast much wider than that, such as wine snobbery and wine jargon, the English pub and the American bar (the barmaid and the barman), noisy cocktail parties, breathalysers, the licensing laws, Alcoholics Anonymous, home brewing, and so on. And on those infrequent occasions when topical additions come on the Drink scene, like the Campaign for Real Ale or Theme Pubs, then the boys are onto them before you can say "Mine's a bitter".

In the main, however, our comic artists tend to stick to the 80 per cent proof essence of what it's all about, which is alcohol and its insidious effects on man. (Or even dogs, as one of Donegan's cartoons will show.) From ffolkes's 14th-century tippling monks to Heath's 20th-century saturated winos, the whole imbibing tableau is there, not quite *in vino veritas* but nearly so. And there are quieter moments, for instance, the Starke cartoon where one chap is saying to his pal, "This is what I like – a nice empty pub. Pity the beer is so bloody awful."

William Hewison
April 1986

"I drink to pluck up the courage to order ridiculous sounding cocktails."

PRONUNCIATION ADVISOR

"Do me a favour! How do you expect me to keep ice in this heat!"

"Begorrah, Dooley, welcome back to the only country in the world where a nun buys a round!"

*"There we are – all gone! See? I wiped all the
hippopotami off the bar."*

"Hallelujah! I'm a born-again drunk!"

"He's the patron saint of drunks!"

"Shylvia, shouldn't 'shinsherely' be shpelled
with a 'shee'?"

"When I get to the aggressive stage, pal, try to remember how much I liked you while I was still maudlin."

"Are you stinko or have you come crawling back to me?"

"*Which size would you like – mild euphoria, tiresome aggressiveness, maudlin self-pity or lying in the gutter?*"

"What are IBM, Xerox and ITT drinking these days, Jack?"

"Sorry, sir – skis must not be worn in the bar."

"Just our luck – the '72 won't reach its best until 1987."

"Poor old Grenville – champagne cork right between the eyes."

"'Go home'? You're asking me to go to a place where ninety per cent of all accidents occur?"

"Oh, yes. Oh, yes. I may be a failed musician, a failed businessman, a failed husband and a failed father. But you better believe I'm one hellava successful drunk."

"My name's Peter Simpson and I'm hovering around in the hope of being drawn into the conversation."

"Sid, this is my boy. I'm introducing him to the booze culture."

"It's been a good life."

"All the other men have mellowed!"

"Was there anything in particular you wanted to talk about? My views on most subjects are as half-baked as the next man's."

''Anybody else doesn't believe in consensus?''

''A friend of mine drank twenty
bottles of this a day and drowned.''

"I sympathise, sir, but I don't think your dog's illness is sufficient reason for me to buy you a drink."

"Oh dear! When Godfrey decides to 'take a stand
on his beliefs' he's not fit to drive home."

"A new breathalyser, gentlemen.
It recognises the grip of fellow masons."

"Regulars? Heavens, no, they're on loan from the Tourist Board."

*"I hope they're not contemplating a modernisation.
This is fresh sawdust."*

"Alice, have you been drinking again?"

"You can come in as long as you behave yourselves.
I don't want you driving my regulars out."

"I see they've tarted up all the pubs in this area."

''*Provisional Salvation Army. Nobody leaves the room till this tin's filled!*''

"Get a move on, Jenkins – that wine doesn't travel very well."

"Usual, Sam?"   *"Please, Bill."*

"Cheers, Sam!"   *"Cheers, Bill!"*

"It's a great library – they all contain bottles."

*"Sooner or later it had to come – a two **bar** family."*

"Really, Henry! That's one drink you could cut down on!"

"Another trouble-maker from the Campaign For Real Shove Ha'penny."

"As newcomers to the community, we'd rather hoped Campari and soda all round would have broken the ice."

*"You should have seen the bird who **used** to work behind the bar . . ."*

"There goes Henderson. I think they're putting something in the Drambuie."

"*Thank you, no, if I have another one now I won't get any praying done.*"

"He's a bloody useless driver as well."

"If they ban drink here, it'll mean the end of cricket as a game."

"Stop moaning – we were at your parents' last year!"

"Starting the Trafalgar Night thrash a bit early, aren't we?"

"He was a child star in the early 'Tarzan's,' but then the talkies came along."

"This one's to help me unwind for the office . . . this one's to wind me up to face the wife and kids . . . this one's to help me unwind after the evening with them . . ."

"Always more interested in saving some for the Derby than enjoying Glyndebourne."

*"How dare you? Did I ask **you** what **you're** drinking?"*

"See? Even the wine waiter doesn't understand me."

"To life, as we know it!"

"OK if I don't bother about the twist? There's nobody here but us."

"What a coincidence! I, too, am celebrating my divorce. We obviously have much in common."

"I'd buy me a drink if I were you! – I get aggressive when I'm sober!"

"In this next song, Schubert laments the fact that his beer keeps sliding off the piano."

"Frankly, I think Napoleon Brandy deserves a better fate."

"... or might I perhaps suggest the Château Margaux '63 with its delicious hints of running naked, laughing, through verdant woods."

"Are you saying that there are people about who can still afford to do both?"

"My first husband used to try to get me drunk."

"I'm warning you for the last time,
Mac. 'Hopefully' is an adverb."

*"No brandy until you've finished
your Pimm's."*

"Have you tried drink?"

*"You wouldn't hit a man wearing
Pierre Cardin fashion eyewear?"*

"Let's face it, anyone can look unsuccessful."

*"The truth is I only drink
to be unsociable."*

"Hang on, the rent was only five swigs of the bottle last week."

"You're going to miss that cold when it goes . . ."

"It was the only way her father could afford the champagne!"

"Same again, Harry!"

"Go home if you must, Sudberry, but you don't look all that sick to me!"

"It takes me about four drinks before I begin to feel like my birth sign!"

"Him? He's my bouncer."

"I drank myself to death – now I'm rather lost for anything to do."

*"The night is young and somewhere inside
my beak I have a bottle of Beaujolais."*

*"Brown ale with meat,
Stanley – **pale** ale with fish."*

"Oh yes! I've met your sort before."

"Will someone take me away from
him – he's turning me into a drunk."

"Or there's a 'Titanic Stopper', gin, brandy, vodka, lots of crushed
ice, dash of Angosturas, always goes down well in the warm
weather, or there again you can have . . ."

"...and three small whiskeys."

"Yes! I'll hijack one of those."

"Drink can do funny things to a man."

"Travels well. Goes through the air like a bullet."

"I'm fighting drunk, pal. Know what that means? My eyes won't focus, my co-ordination is shot, and I may fall down at any moment. So watch it."

*"You'll find that Amanda's
parsnip wine will happily
complement the delicate flavour
of the nut cutlet."*

"Our distinguished prosecutor here has made a very strong case against the Irish. I now call the first witness for the defence!"

"You don't _look_ eighteen."

"I owe it all to my dear Mary. Without her, I would undoubtedly have landed in the gutter long ago."

"I think everybody's filling up before the Budget."

"... And a sausage and a small Scotch for him."

"They said, 'You'll never succeed in that parish.' They said, 'You'll never make an impression on that tight-lipped bunch of Puritans.' They said, 'You'll never find the key to the wine cupboard.' Well, two out of three 'ain't bad."

"Don't worry about him, sir – he's a millionaire eccentric."

"One look at you and I said, 'Now here's a guy who's not going to fool around with silly opening one-liners'."

"It's either Matins or Evensong but who cares?"

"*Due to popular demand, you now have a choice of hard liquor, wine, beer, or several non-alcoholic beverages.*"

"It's either Matins or Evensong but who cares?"

"Due to popular demand, you now have a choice of hard liquor,
wine, beer, or several non-alcoholic beverages."

*"When Kirsten serves the wine nobody cares **what's** in the bottle."*

"This is what I like – a nice empty pub. Pity the beer is so bloody awful."

"We're not good enough for him now he's gone and ridden a winner or two!"

"Oh God no! Not the '23!"

"Well, you wanted a typical English pub."

"Congratulations, sir! You're about to become the ten-thousandth visitor to this village to buy its oldest inhabitants a pint!"

"*It's a pity he doesn't write. He could have been another Scott Fitzgerald.*"

"While you're in the cellar, would you get me a bottle of Moet & Chandon?"

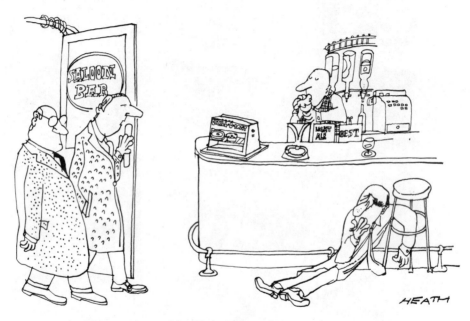

*"I see they've redesigned the old place – he used
to be in the other bar."*

*"At least the magic hasn't gone out of the
Newcastle Brown, thank God!"*

*"Worked out rather well on the whole . . . chap next door wanted
a Steinway and I wanted a bar."*

"I've given up Lent."

"I came here years ago as a social worker. I liked it so much I've been here ever since."

"*Classic post-natal depression – got hit with a paternity suit this morning.*"

"We must try this collective bargaining thing again sometime soon."

*"To be honest, I thought I was gate-crashing a
different kind of party."*

"I'm tired of telling people, we don't have draught bitter any more because there's no demand for it."

"*I think we've come up with a wonderful new keg bitter –*
80,000 rats can't be wrong."

*"Don't worry about giving short measure – it is our duty to
protect them from dangerous driving."*

"I told you there was no need to bring our own booze."

"Never touch the water myself – stick to the old vin rouge, I always say."

"Yes, I'm on Social Security . . . No, I've never done a hand's
turn in my life . . . Yes, I'm of Irish extraction . . ."

"You know what I like about this monastery? It makes religion attractive."

"*It's the dreaded Campaign for Real Flowers.*"

"I still don't like it."

"Every week for a hundred and fifty years we used to hold our meetings next door and then last week we discovered this place."

"Of course, my romance is really with the grape."

*"Mynheer Rubens,
some gentlemen to
see you."*

"That bottle of light ale is a sign of the times."

*"For a time Brother Sebastian was exposed to the follies
of the world outside."*

"I wish you'd stop going on about good honest English bitter."

"Of course, the drink ruined him as a stuntman."

*"Nearest the bull has to drive
us home."*

"*I think there is something wrong when our only social asset is that we are early arrivers.*"

"I might have known – a flaming woman driver!!"

"He used to have one of the best acts in the business."

"Who ordered the large Pernod?"

*"I just knew it was a good site, so
I applied for the franchise."*

*"To be perfectly honest, Harcroft, I shan't be sorry when this
Real Ale craze is over."*

*"Hey, Sarge – they say they all
want to give a urine sample."*

"*Mr Tomkins wanted on the telephone. Is there a Mr Tomkins here please.*"

"*It annoys me when they come in just to use the spittoon.*"

"You don't fool me – I know you're off to the pub . . ."